The Ruin And The Resurrection

Poems from the Edges of Silence

Sonali Baksi

India | USA | UK

Copyright © Sonali Baksi
All Rights Reserved.

This book has been self-published with all reasonable efforts taken to make the material error-free by the author. No part of this book shall be used, reproduced in any manner whatsoever without written permission from the author, except in the case of brief quotations embodied in critical articles and reviews.

The Author of this book is solely responsible and liable for its content including but not limited to the views, representations, descriptions, statements, information, opinions, and references ["Content"]. The Content of this book shall not constitute or be construed or deemed to reflect the opinion or expression of the Publisher or Editor. Neither the Publisher nor Editor endorse or approve the Content of this book or guarantee the reliability, accuracy, or completeness of the Content published herein and do not make any representations or warranties of any kind, express or implied, including but not limited to the implied warranties of merchantability, fitness for a particular purpose.

The Publisher and Editor shall not be liable whatsoever...

Made with ❤ on the BookLeaf Publishing Platform
www.bookleafpub.in
www.bookleafpub.com

Dedication

For love in all the ways it arrives, stays, and leaves.

Preface

The Ruin and the Resurrection is a collection born from silence, from words that stayed behind when the moment to speak had already passed. Each poem began as a fragment of thought, a reflection of love, distance, and the spaces between people where emotion quietly lingers.

These poems are not addressed to anyone in particular, yet they belong to everyone who has ever felt deeply but remained quiet, who has loved without confession, or who has carried memories like folded letters in the heart. Writing this collection became a form of release, a way of giving voice to emotions that resist conclusion. In these pages, love is not always gentle, nor is loss always tragic. Sometimes it is simply the way life unfolds, imperfect, beautiful, and unfinished.

This book is not meant to provide answers, but rather to hold space for feeling. If you find yourself somewhere in these lines, know that you were never alone in your silence.

Acknowledgements

This book began as a whisper, a collection of thoughts I never found the courage to say aloud. It grew from late-night reflections, quiet heartbreaks, and the kind of love that lingers long after it's gone. To those who have crossed my path, whether you stayed or became a memory, thank you. Every encounter, every silence, every goodbye has shaped the words within these pages. To my friends and family, who offered warmth, patience, and belief when I doubted my own. To the readers who find pieces of themselves in these letters, this book now belongs to you. May you find comfort in knowing that some emotions, even when unspoken, still connect us all. And finally, to love, in all its forms. Thank you for teaching me to feel, to break, and to write.

1. Home

Home,
A word so small,
Yet vast in emotion's sway,
My youngerself,
In disbelief,
Would question my today,
For now, my heart does yearn,
To find it's homely way.

Home just four letters,
In travels wide and journeys far,
My soul has lessons learned,
Redeemed,
And when exhaustion grips my bones,
To home,
My heart is yearned.

Home, one syllable,
Where peaceful dreams glide,
In it's gentle, soothing tide,

And no night's haunting fears here,
With home's warm hearth's embrace,
My heart forever shall reside.

2. The Ruin in Me

There are days I wake with tenderness in my chest,
a heart that only ever meant to love,
to pour, to give, to cradle,
and yet, somehow,
everything I touch bruises a little.
I tell myself I am kind.
I tell myself I mean well.
But love, when filtered through my fears,
becomes a storm disguised as devotion.
There's a ruin in me,
quiet, deliberate,
the kind that smiles while it breaks things.
And after every silence I create,
I taste it,
that faint, bitter trace,
like the bottom of a teacup
that once held warmth.
It hurts to know the villain
doesn't always come wearing another face.
Sometimes she wears mine,

eyes soft, heart full,
hands trembling with sincerity,
still capable of protecting everything
she once swore to protect.

3. Serendipity

Time, the endless archivist of dust and bones, could have fled us in separate volumes,
left our pages to yellow in solitude.
Yet, in its rare mercy, it bent the arc of chance,
threaded my hours through the eye of your years,
and set us down in the same season of the same world.
Think of all the countless births and quiet endings,
all the oceans where we might have drowned alone,
all the wars of sky and soil we might have missed each other by,
And still, here we are.
How fortunate to walk the same trembling earth,
to exist beside you,
to sip the same light from the same sun's old hand,
to live where your voice can cross, the small distance to mine.
If existence is an accident,
Let me be grateful for this most exquisite mistake.

4. Kinder Sea

I wish you laughter that comes uninvited,
Like a bird landing on your hand,
And love that stays quiet, steady,
Like the sea against the sand.
I wish you courage when the waters turn cold,
A heart that still believes in spring,
I wish your days to bend like photons,
Through lenses of hope and wonder,
Where gravity only pulls you toward what is meant for you,
And may entropy never steals your order,
But teach you how to bloom through chaos.
I wish you kinder sea, my love,
Not one without storms,
But one that always brings you home,
A quantum of peace in every wave,
A chemistry of warmth in every touch,
And a physics of forever between your heart and mine,
And the quiet constant of our bond,
A force no universe could unwrite.

6. Anatomy of jealousy

Jealousy is not always born from malice.
Sometimes, it's simply love afraid of its own shadow,
a tremor in the heart that asks, "Am I still seen?"

It is a two-edged sword,
cutting both the one who feels it and the one it's felt for.
It wounds with comparison,
but it also sharpens awareness
that what we fear to lose
must have mattered deeply.
It is two sides of the same coin:
on one lies devotion, on the other, doubt.
Both spun from the same hand,
both belonging to the same heart.

Jealousy makes us helpless
because it speaks in the language of imagination,
we suffer more in what we picture than in what is real.
Yet, beneath its restlessness lies a strange truth:
to be jealous is to still care,

to still wish for belonging.

Perhaps that is why love tolerates it,
not as a flaw, but as proof
that it is human, imperfect, alive.
So I do not curse jealousy anymore.
I hold it like fire,
close enough to feel its warmth,
but far enough to remember
it can burn.

7. The Quiet Crossroads

There are days the world feels heavy,
not like a burden, but a question,
asking who I am when I'm no longer sure
what I'm running toward.

The struggle is not always loud.
Sometimes it's the quiet ache
of choosing between comfort and calling,
between what feeds the soul
and what pays for its hunger.

Love, too, stands uncertain at the gate,
a tender mirage that feels real enough to stay,
yet fades when I reach for it
with hands trembling from old betrayals.

Friendship, that fragile truce
between hearts that mean well
and silences that mean nothing,
teaches me that even trust

has its seasons of drought and bloom.

I walk through each day like a crossroads,
carrying maps written by other people's dreams,
wondering which turn is truly mine.
And yet, somewhere between loss and learning,
I find that struggle is its own kind of faith,
a belief that even confusion is sacred,
that we are becoming
precisely through what we cannot yet name.

8. Friendship

They say friends are important,
I say they are vital,
For what is existence
without a soul that walks beside you
in silence and in storm?

What worth is a bond
If it is not like Draupadi and Krishna,
woven by trust that no fire could consume,
or like Karna and Duryodhan,
where loyalty defied reason,
and even in certain defeat,
You stand unshaken, unashamed.

What meaning has friendship
if it cannot transcend the walls of wealth and want,
like Sudama and Krishna,
where a humble gift
outweighed kingdoms,
And simplicity sang the song of love eternal?

What friendship is it
If it never stirred you beyond your confines,
If it never held a mirror to your being
and showed you not what you wished to see,
But what you truly were?

For they say,
You are born to your parents,
bound by fate to your kin,
and even love, perhaps,
is written upon the stars.
But friends,
Friends are the choice of the soul.
A covenant carved by will,
not by destiny.

And once chosen,
You sail together,
through tempests and time,
through laughter and loss,
upon the same fragile vessel of trust.
For friendship is no mere bond,
It is the quiet defiance of solitude,
the sacred bridge
between what we are
and what we dare to become.

9. The art of letting go

When I was young,
I searched for resonance,
a matching frequency of heartbeats,
a soul oscillating in perfect phase with mine,
a love bound not by chance,
but by the symmetry of destiny's equation.
I imagined affection as fusion,
two atoms colliding,
releasing light enough
to outshine every darkness.
I mistook that brilliance for eternity.
But as life unfolded,
entropy set in.
Order gave way to understanding.
The illusions, once crystalline and pure,
fractured under the pressure of truth,
like glass under too much gravity.
The fairy tales I adored
were chemical reactions that could never sustain,
their energy dissipated,

their bonds too unstable
to endure time's corrosion.
And now, curiously,
I no longer crave that reaction.
Love feels less like necessity,
more like a distant star,
its light still reaching me,
though the source has long since died.
Perhaps this is evolution,
a quiet adaptation of the soul.
To no longer seek external warmth,
but to generate it within,
self-sustaining,
like a star learning its own fusion.

And now strangely,
Suddenly,
I don't crave love anymore.
It feels foreign to me,
Though once it was the only language
I longed to speak.
How strange to be emptied of the very thing
That once defined me.

10. What's Meant to Return

That day, we spoke of destiny,
How what is truly yours
will always find its way back,
how love, if real,
moves with its own gravity,
never losing direction,
only taking the long way home.

And yet, if you never return,
I will take it as the universe's soft whisper,
that you were meant to be
a beautiful constellation in my sky,
not the cosmos itself.
Some souls are comets, not planets,
they pass through your orbit,
ignite your silence,
and leave you staring upward
long after their light has gone.
They do not belong to permanence,
but to wonder.

Still, I hope life wraps you in warmth,
that every sunrise feels kind,
that time bends gently around your joy.
And perhaps,
somewhere between the stars,
where memory outlives time,
You will feel it,
a pulse, faint yet familiar,
a heart that still softens
at the thought of you,
not in longing,
but in quiet gratitude,
for having once known
What the universe sounds like
when it speaks in your name.

11. The Eternal Equation

They say love is theatre,
all light and noise,
curtains rising to applause and spectacle.
But mine,
mine is a silent vow,
I can die for you in silence,
a devotion unseen, unrecorded,
eternal as breath.

You once asked,
"Is love truly the only thing you think about?"
And perhaps it is,
for it was the only seed
that ever took root in me.
From the first flicker of youth,
I never longed for gold or grandeur,
only for a heart
That would recognize mine.

To me, love was never a pastime nor a performance,

It was the warmth of a door opening
after a long winter,
It was the pulse beneath silence,
the prayer behind breath,
the unnamed force
that keeps the stars from falling apart.

12. The Quiet Law of Love

If it were you,
If it meant being with you
for even the briefest flicker of eternity,
I would abandon the world
without a breath of hesitation.
For what are tomorrows
to a soul that has once
tasted forever?

Real love,
the kind that trembles the soul
and hushes the world into stillness,
It is never a mistake.
It asks for no reason,
seeks no reward.
It is both the wound and the balm,
the ache and the awakening,
the birth and the undoing.

And if I must lose everything

to feel it only once,
I would still choose it,
again and again,
in every lifetime, written or unwritten.
To have loved,
wholly and without armor,
is to have lived,
even if only
for the quiet span
of your name
upon my lips.

13. The Space Between Us

I wasn't your first love,
and somewhere between what we were
and what we lost,
the world unfolded in ways we never planned.
We drifted apart,
not out of choice,
but through the quiet weight of life
and all the unspoken things that stood between us.
I left,
thinking distance would make forgetting easier,
but it only carved your name deeper
into the places I thought were empty.
In that space of silence,
I realised, we were never meant to end,
We were meant to find our way back stronger,
more aware of what it means to stay.
Yes, there are trust issues,
scars that ache when touched,
but even through the cracks,
our love breathes,

steady and stubborn,
refusing to die.
So this time,
I am not asking for forever to come easily.
I am willing to build it,
piece by piece,
with patience, with faith,
with you.
I wasn't your first love,
but I intend to be your last,
the quiet that follows the storm,
the hand you still reach for
when all else fades,
No matter how long that takes.

14. Had Time Been Softer

I often wonder
If love ever truly ends,
or if it simply changes form,
quietly folding itself
into the places we no longer reach.
Perhaps it lingers
not as longing,
But as understanding.

If we never speak again,
I would like to think
You'll remember me
not as the one who stayed,
nor the one who left,
But as the one who tried
to meet love with both hands open,
unafraid of its uncertainty,
unafraid of its cost.
There was a time
When I believed love could bend time,

that devotion could rewrite distance,
That wanting was enough to make something last.
But the years have taught me otherwise:
that even love must obey impermanence,
that even tenderness has its own season
of decay and renewal.

We were not undone by absence,
But by the quiet truth
That not all things are meant to endure.
Some arrive only to awaken us,
to teach us where the heart ends
and where the self begins.
Still, I carry no bitterness.
Only a kind of gratitude,
for the moments when the world was softer,
for the way your presence shaped
the contours of my becoming.

And if time had been gentler,
Perhaps we might have stayed.
But then, we would never have learned
that love's truest form
is not in possession,
But in release.
So if you ever think of me,
I hope it is with calm recognition,

That's what we were
was neither a failure nor a loss,
but a chapter of awakening,
a necessary crossing
on the long road
back to ourselves.

15. In Love's Tangled Web

In love's tangled web,
We often mistake the pull of pain for passion,
the ache for depth,
the chaos for something worth keeping.
But not every fire warms,
Some only burn to remind us
How fragile we've become.
Flee from the man who brings misery,
the one who makes you question
the softness of your own heart.
For the love that demands your silence,
that thrives on your uncertainty,
is not love,
It is hunger wearing a familiar face.

He will draw out your darkest side,
mirror your fears until you no longer recognize
the person you were before him.
You will call it a connection,
until you learn

That real love never asks you
to dim your light
just to make another feel whole.

There is a quiet power
in walking away,
In choosing peace over apology,
in reclaiming the fragments
of yourself you once gave away too easily.
In time,
You will see,
that love is not meant to consume,
but to expand;
not to bind,
But to free.

True happiness will not arrive
in grand confessions or desperate pleas,
but in the steady presence
of someone who sees you,
not as something to fix,
But as something already whole.
And when you find that love,
You will rise,
not because they lift you,
but because, in their presence,

You finally remember
How to stand tall again.

16. what makes you happy

What makes you happy
doesn't have to stand on reason's edge,
doesn't need a name,
or a witness to nod in approval.

It may be a quiet sunrise
over a cracked rooftop,
a song you hum to no one,
a dream that never learned to explain itself.

Let the world demand logic,
You owe it none.
Joy is not a thesis,
nor a confession.

It is the secret pulse
beneath your ribs,
the moment your soul sighs,
"Yes, this is mine."

What makes you happy
may appear absurd,
but perhaps absurdity
is how truth disguises itself,
too wild for reason to cage.

So cradle it gently,
that tender, unreasonable light;
Do not ask it to justify its glow.
Let it burn
in its own strange language,
and trust that the fire knows
Why it chose you.

17. When Death Comes

I don't want to die
the death that doesn't smell,
the kind that leaves no trace
of having lived.
I want the air to remember me,
the way it remembers rain,
or burnt incense,
or salt from a wept ocean.

When death comes,
I hope I am not bargaining for more.
I hope my hands are open,
not clutching at what was never mine.
Let there be fewer complaints,
more gratitude for the cracks
that let the light in.

I want to meet death
like an old friend arriving late,
to smile,

to say, "I was waiting,
But I lived while I waited."
Let my heart be soft,
My regrets are few,
My joy is unmeasured.

And when death comes,
I hope I am ready,
not because I am finished,
But because I have finally learned
to stop holding back.

18. I Might Love Again

I might love again,
But I won't fall in love again.
I've learned that love need not be a plunge,
It can be a slow return,
a gentle remembering of warmth
without surrendering the self to fire.

I might trust again,
But I won't get blinded again.
I've seen how easily devotion
turns into disappearance,
How, in trying to belong,
We often forget where we begin.

I might open my heart,
But I'll keep a room that's mine alone,
a quiet corner untouched by need,
where peace sits unbothered
by the comings and goings of love.

I might dream again,
but not forever,
only moments that breathe honesty,
of eyes that meet without hunger,
of touch that doesn't claim to heal.

I might forgive again,
But I won't forget the lessons
etched by ache and distance.
For every wound I carry
has taught me the shape of my own strength,
and how to stand,
not waiting to be chosen,
but choosing, at last,
myself.

19. When you stop forcing

Life flows easier than you think,
when you stop wrestling the current,
when you let the water know your name
and trust it to carry you home.

All that you've been chasing
was never running away;
it was waiting, quietly,
for you to be still enough to see.

It's not about control,
the river has its own intelligence,
the tide its ancient memory.
Your part is to listen,
to unclench the hand
that's gripping what must go.
Alignment is not earned;
it's revealed
when resistance softens.

Life flows easier
when you forgive yourself,
for the detours, the delays,
for trying too hard to be the light
instead of letting it through.
And when you do,
you find the current gentle,
the path clear,
the world already in tune
with the rhythm you had forgotten
was your own.

20. Purpose

I knew from the beginning,
there was no future carved for us,
no promise waiting at the end of our words.
Still, I let the hours unfold,
let my heart wander into forbidden rooms
where your presence felt like meaning.
The mind warns,
but the heart listens to no reason.
It craves the ache,
the almost,
the impossible.
I never wanted us to become
a tangled story of almost and never-was,
captives to what the world would not allow.

But some things are like sand,
the tighter you hold them,
the faster they slip through,
leaving behind
the weight of absence.

So I stood still,
watching the slow undoing of myself,
my heart splintering quietly,
my thoughts collapsing into smoke,
my desires turning against me,
devouring what they once adored.

It felt cruel,
How love always chose the wrong face to wear,
how it arrived, only to remind me
What I could never keep.
But pain, too, has its own strange purpose.
You were my necessary evil,
the chaos that gave shape
to my emptiness.
Through you,
I learned that love does not always heal.
sometimes it wounds to awaken.

You made me believe again,
that even broken hearts remember how to beat,
that even after the fire,
something in us still reaches for warmth.
And maybe next time,
I won't fall in love,
maybe I'll rise into it,
knowing that love,

like pain,
is not meant to destroy,
but to return us
to ourselves.

21. The Child in You

May you fall in love
with someone who speaks your language,
so you don't spend a lifetime
translating your soul into fragments
that no one listens to.

May you never have to dim your light
just to be understood.
May your silence still feel like poetry
to the one who truly sees you.

May you not lose the child in you,
the one who still believes in magic,
who laughs without reason,
who holds wonder
like it's something sacred.

May life get softer when someone holds your hand,
not spiral into confusion and noise.
May love be your calm, not your chaos.

May it anchor you,
not drown you.

May you remember,
you are special,
even on the days when you feel invisible.
Even when your name echoes back as emptiness.

May you never beg for love,
for attention, for worth.
May you know that being yourself
was always enough.
And when the world forgets your radiance,
may you remind yourself gently,
the right souls never need translation,
they arrive already fluent
in the language of you.

22. I Hope One Day

I hope one day you gather the courage
to walk toward the very things that once made you
tremble,
to face every monster you ever named in fear,
and see that most of them lived within you,
waiting to be tamed by love.

I hope one day you no longer let hesitation
become the thief of your destiny,
that when the door opens,
you step through, even if your hands are shaking.

I hope one day you learn the art of kindness,
not from the world,
but from the quiet ache of your own heart,
and treat others
as you once wished to be treated when no one did.

I hope someday you find arms
that do not complete you,

but honour what was already whole;
arms that hold you
like a prayer that has finally been answered.

I hope someday you meet a soul
who brings light to the forgotten corridors within you,
someone whose laughter
awakens the sleeping parts of your joy,
and whose silence
teaches you the eloquence of peace.

I hope someday you understand,
Life is not a battle to be won,
but a journey to be witnessed.
And yet, by enduring,
You have already prevailed.

I hope one day you never again
Apologise for being the person
Your journey required you to become.

I hope one day forgiveness finds you,
for those who wronged you,
and for the ways you wronged yourself.

I hope someday you see your worth
not as a measure,

but as a light,
unchanging, infinite, whole.

And above all,
I hope someday you love yourself
with the same tenderness
The Divine had
When it first imagined you.

www.ingramcontent.com/pod-product-compliance
Lightning Source LLC
Chambersburg PA
CBHW070500050426
42449CB00012B/3064